W9-AJP-989

DATE DUE

AU

AF

E PATEL
Patel, Andrea
Onthatday

35000093096542 Children's

onthatday
a book of hope for children
by andrea patel

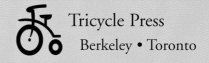

Tricycle Press
Berkeley • Toronto

Text and illustrations copyright © 2001 by Andrea Patel

All rights reserved. No part of this book may be reproduced in any form
without the written permission of the publisher, except in the case
of brief quotations embodied in critical articles or reviews.

Tricycle Press
a little division of Ten Speed Press
P.O. Box 7123, Berkeley, California 94707
www.tenspeed.com

Originally published in December 2001 by Star Root Press,
Austerlitz, New York, www.starrootpress.com

Cover design by Jean Sanchirico
Typeset in Adobe Garamond
The illustrations in this book were rendered in tissue paper collage.

Library of Congress Control Number: 2001099138
ISBN 1-58246-100-7

First Tricycle Press printing, 2002
Printed in the United States of America

1 2 3 4 5 6 — 06 05 04 03 02

In memory of those who lost their lives
on September 11, 2001

The world is blue.

The world is green.

The world is bright.

Is there anything we can do to make the world right again?

Yes. Whether you're three years old, or thirteen years old,
or thirty years old, or one-hundred-and-three years old, you can help.

The world is very big, and really round, and pretty peaceful.

But one day a terrible thing happened.

The world, which had been blue and green and bright and very big and

really round and pretty peaceful, got badly hurt.

Many people were injured. Many other people died. And everyone was sad.

Sometimes bad things happen in nature, things like tornadoes
or earthquakes or fires.

But sometimes bad things happen because people act
in mean ways and hurt each other on purpose. That's what happened
on that day, a day when it felt like the world broke. This is scary,
and hard to understand, even for grown-ups.

You can help by sharing.

You can help by playing and laughing.

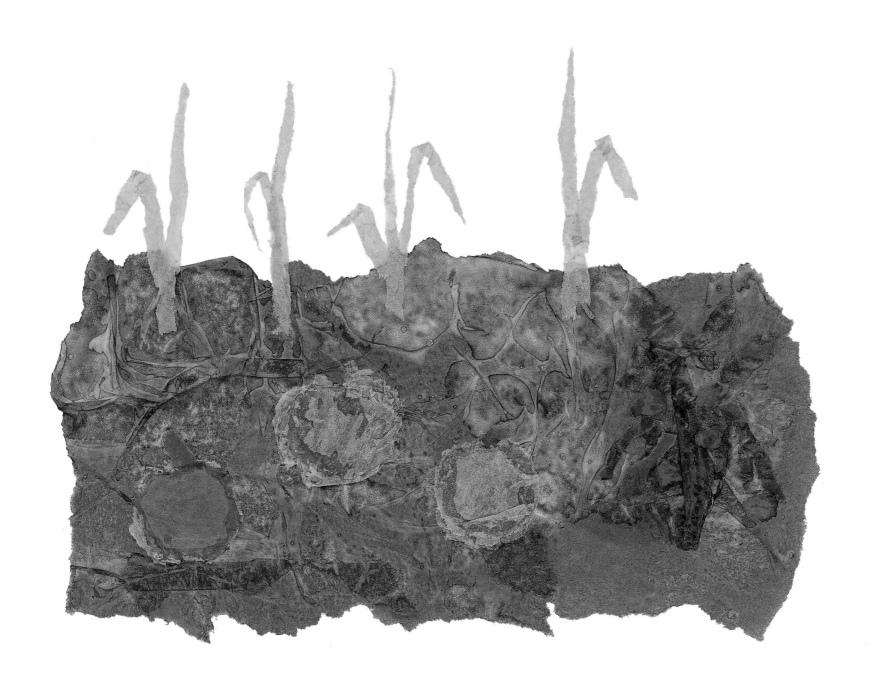

You can help by taking good care of the Earth.

You can help by being kind to people.

When bad things happen, only a small piece of the world breaks,
not the whole world. Goodness is in the world, and it's stronger than badness.
There will always be good things in the world.
You are one of those good things.

Author's Note

The world stopped making sense to me on September 11.

A week later, still dazed, I found myself sitting quietly. Unexpectedly, words began to come into my head—words with cadence, words with page turns, words that swam around and around and around inside of me. They stayed in my mind, growing louder and more insistent. Eventually I wrote them down. Writing was a cathartic act, but once the words were out, they were forgotten. Two weeks later I found the paper. As I reread it, my head became flooded with images. Like the words, these too demanded representation on paper. I acquiesced. Thus the book became my attempt to make sense again of the world at a simpler level, with a preschooler's understanding.

Claudia Ricci, founder of Star Root Press, leaped fearlessly into the unknown by publishing the first edition of this book. I am grateful beyond words for her commitment and belief. I was also fortunate to have colleagues who gave me feedback and encouragement; their help in shaping this book is genuinely appreciated. The entire Oberlin crew listened, commented, questioned, critiqued, but most of all supported; thanks to all of you. I owe much to Ellie Hayford Atwater and Maria Whalen, who gave me clearheaded criticism as well as endless classroom latitude; and to Rob Peterson, who offered his immediate, full, and continued support. I am deeply grateful to Kathy Clausen, whose clarity of vision helps me find my own; Paula Hellman, whose wise counsel always illuminates; and Deborah Zecher, whose multiple roles as spiritual architect, matchmaker, and centerboard helped facilitate this book from beginning to end. There is no way to adequately thank Florence Liberman, my mother, and Gail Ullman, my sister, who picked up the many pieces of my daily life that I let go; or my children, Toby, Monica, Jesse, and Gabe, whose wholehearted support of this venture meant that they had to live with a fully distracted mother. Finally, my deepest thanks go to Dan, my husband, whose love provides the secure foundation supporting all I do.

Andrea Patel has been a teacher for twelve years. Trained as a musician, metalsmith, and pastry chef, she has had a lifelong involvement in the arts. She lives with her family in western Massachusetts. *on that day* is her first book.